STUDY GUIDE
FOR INDIVIDUAL OR GROUP

C000203281

Approaching
Jesus

Cathy Madavan

CWR

Acknowledgements

Writing is a solitary sport, but one which is only made possible by your team. I would like to thank Mark, my theological, proof-reading, family-juggling husband for making it possible; Naomi and Izzy for coping so brilliantly with Mum being absent or totally distracted and for the Locks Heath Free Church family who provided many lifts and much encouragement. It is a pleasure and a privilege to write with the CWR team and I thank God for the opportunity and pray that every reader will be as encouraged as I have been along the way.

Copyright © CWR, 2014

Previously published by CWR as a *Cover to Cover Lent Study Guide*, Waverley Abbey House, Waverley Lane, Farnham, Surrey GU9 8EP, UK. Registered Charity No. 294387. Registered Limited Company No. 1990308. Reprinted 2016. This version published 2017 by CWR. Reprinted 2018.

The right of Cathy Madavan to be identified as the author of this work has been asserted by her in accordance with the Copyright, Designs and Patents Act 1988, sections 77 and 78.

www.cathymadavan.com

Twitter: @cathymadavan

Facebook: Cathy Madavan Speaker/Presenter/Writer page

For list of National Distributors visit cwr.org.uk/distributors

Unless otherwise indicated, all Scripture references are from the Holy Bible: New International Version (Anglicised edition) Copyright © 1979, 1984, 2011 by Biblica (formerly International Bible Society). Used by permission of Hodder & Stoughton Publishers, a Hachette UK company. All rights reserved. 'NIV' is a registered trademark of Biblica (formerly International Bible Society). UK trademark number 1448790.

Concept development, editing, design and production by CWR.

Photographs: Fotosearch, istockphoto.com

Printed in the UK by Linney Group

ISBN: 978-1-78259-737-7

Contents

4 Introduction

7 STUDY | **ONE**
The Pharisees: A Passion for Purity Matthew 15:1–20

16 STUDY | **TWO**
A Father: A Persistent Prayer Matthew 17:14–22

25 STUDY | **THREE**
Peter: A Question of Forgiveness Matthew 18:21–35

34 STUDY | **FOUR**
A Rich Man and a Generous Woman:
A Beautiful Thing Matthew 19:16-26; Matthew 26:6–13

44 STUDY | **FIVE**
Judas: A Hidden Agenda Matthew 26:47–54

53 STUDY | **SIX**
Mary and Mary: A Restoration Project Matthew 28:1–10

62 Leader's Notes

Introduction

In this series of studies, we will be spending some time together looking through the eyes of some very different people who approached Jesus in the Gospel of Matthew. But hopefully, more than that, it is my genuine prayer that during these weeks, each of us will take this time to approach Jesus for ourselves again.

This is a wonderful opportunity for us all to refocus our minds and reorientate our busy lives towards our Saviour Jesus, however easy or difficult we might find that at the moment. During the forty days in the wilderness, Jesus was tempted and tested but above all He demonstrated a powerful understanding of who He was, and what mattered most to Him. As we start week one, we can enter these forty days of reflection and focus by stripping back a little of our internal clutter and external clatter to make way for more of Jesus in our lives. We too, amidst our tests and temptations, need a greater realisation of *who* we are in God and what really matters to us in light of that.

While studying the Gospels to prepare for writing this guide, I was encouraged to read that, time and time again, Jesus approached people. He was constantly calling, walking, explaining, touching, sharing meals and welcoming. And, of course, He still does. However, as we will discover, there were also people who took the initiative and approached Jesus – with all kinds of pressures, personalities, influences, agendas and needs. And, of course, we still do.

We don't come to Jesus in a hermetically sealed and sanctified container, impervious to the stresses and strains of life, and immune to disappointment – with circumstances, other people or with ourselves. And if we are really honest, we also sometimes come to God with confusion about His ways and frustration about His purposes. Thank goodness the scriptures are filled with examples of normal people who approach and interact with Jesus just like we do!

There are many examples of people who approached Jesus in the Gospels (and I hope you will find the time to read through

Matthew, or any Gospel, and find the others not included in this guide), but one thing united them all: as they approached and spent time with Jesus, they recognised more and more about God and saw their lives in a new perspective. Some didn't like that perspective and couldn't take on board all that they were hearing. Others, recognising the truth about themselves and the reality of the kingdom of God being revealed before their very eyes, allowed Jesus to reshape their lives.

For us today, the Holy Spirit is still revealing the mystery and the majesty of God to us through Jesus – who is now interceding on our behalf. We too, in His presence, can also recognise the truth about ourselves and see our lives in the light of the kingdom of God. It is with deep gratitude that we can each approach Jesus knowing we are accepted, loved and forgiven because of all that He has done for us through His life, death and resurrection.

It is remarkable, isn't it?

And yet, how do we *really* feel about approaching the King of the universe? I don't know about you, but I approach different people with different feelings. I might be intimidated by one person's power, or nervous about somebody else's intentions; I might be excited about relaxing with a friend or be yearning to be with my family after a trip away from home. It is my hope that by witnessing how these different people approached Jesus, we will be reminded again (and again!) that we can approach Jesus with confidence. We don't need to fear His presence, and we can be assured again that He is completely aware of our needs and desires.

Hebrews 4:14–16

Therefore, since we have a great high priest who has ascended into heaven, Jesus the Son of God, let us hold firmly to the faith we profess. For we do not have a high priest who is unable to empathise with our weaknesses, but we have one who has been tempted in every way, just as we are – yet he did not sin. Let us then approach God's throne of grace with confidence, so that we may receive mercy and find grace to help us in our time of need.

Prayer will be an important part of this time together. It is m prayer that we will all grow in our depth of knowledge and intimacy with Jesus in these coming days. So, before we go a further, whether you are using this book alone or in a group it would be good to take a moment to invite the Holy Spirit lead us as we approach Jesus, both individually and togethei as His disciples.

(Please note, in the prayers and exercises I have used the term 'we', but if you are studying this guide alone please do read this as 'I'.)

Lord, we approach You with grateful hearts for all You have done in our lives. Our desire is to know You more as we spe time in Your presence. In Jesus' name. Amen.

The Pharisees:
A Passion for Purity

Matthew 15:1–20

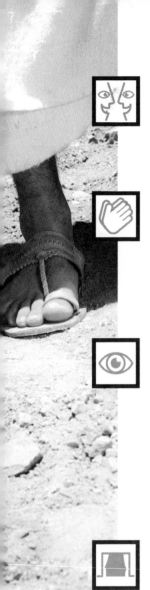

Warm Up

Spend a few minutes tasting something that looks one way on the outside and another on the inside. It might be chocolate or sweets, or a fruit like a pomegranate or a pineapple. What foods are most surprising considering their first impressions?

Opening Prayer

Lord, we pray You would create in us a pure heart today. We don't want to look one way on the outside but be different on the inside. Reveal to us where we need new direction, new energy or a new start, and help us to approach You with a real desire to be holy as You are holy. We don't want to have a religion of rules, but a relationship with You. In the name of Jesus we pray. Amen.

Eye Opener

There's nothing super about superficiality. We can say we are fine to the people at church, we can go to prayer meetings, and we can even serve or give generously without changing our attitudes and reactions. With social media as a tool we can even give others the impression that our life is one long, fun 'selfie' opportunity! But who are we trying to impress and why? Let's reflect and take a real inventory of our spiritual life and our character development. God has plans for us that are more 'super' than we can ask for or imagine.

Setting the Scene

The Pharisees don't have great PR do they? But we are over-simplifying who they are if we just casually regard them all as the 'bad guys' of the Gospels. After all, it is perfectly possible to be religious and zealous but still miss the point, and I sometimes wonder if there is a bit of Pharisee in us all about 'the way we do things'.

In the passage we are about to read, these Pharisees have travelled some distance from Jerusalem to Galilee to approach Jesus. It doesn't appear at this point that they are deliberately trying to trap Jesus, but they are clearly confused by His teaching and they are defensive about their faith, which was a totally all-encompassing life of dedication with a passion for purity.

But what kind of purity? Their layers of traditions, laws and regulations had become their religion – a long way away from the grace and faith filled relationship their forefather Abraham shared with God. In many ways, the outward systems of their religion had totally obscured the heart of God.

They approached Jesus for an answer to their question, not knowing that Jesus was about to shock their understanding and shake their motives.

He does that to us all from time to time doesn't He?
But how do we respond?

Bible Readings

Matthew 15:1–20
Then some Pharisees and teachers of the law came to Jesus from Jerusalem and asked, 'Why do your disciples break the tradition of the elders? They don't wash their hands before they eat!'

Jesus replied, 'And why do you break the command of God for the sake of your tradition? For God said, "Honour your father and mother" and "Anyone who curses their father or mother is to be put to death." But you say that if anyone declares that what might have been used to help their father or mother is "devoted to God," they are not to "honour their father or mother" with it. Thus you nullify the word of God for the sake of your tradition. You hypocrites! Isaiah was right when he prophesied about you:

'"These people honour me with their lips, but their hearts are far from me.

'"They worship me in vain; their teachings are merely human rules."'

Jesus called the crowd to him and said, 'Listen and understand. What goes into someone's mouth does not

defile them, but what comes out of their mouth, that is what defiles them.'

Then the disciples came to him and asked, 'Do you know that the Pharisees were offended when they heard this?'

He replied, 'Every plant that my heavenly Father has not planted will be pulled up by the roots. Leave them; they are blind guides. If the blind lead the blind, both will fall into a pit.'

Peter said, 'Explain the parable to us.'

'Are you still so dull?' Jesus asked them. 'Don't you see that whatever enters the mouth goes into the stomach and then out of the body? But the things that come out of a person's mouth come from the heart, and these defile them. For out of the heart come evil thoughts – murder, adultery, sexual immorality, theft, false testimony, slander. These are what defile a person; but eating with unwashed hands does not defile them.'

Old Testament Connection
1 Samuel 15:22

But Samuel replied: 'Does the Lord delight in burnt offerings and sacrifices as much as in obeying the Lord?

To obey is better than sacrifice, and to heed is better than the fat of rams.'

Session Focus

When we moved to a new church ten years ago, it was becau my husband was to be their new minister. I think we spent t best part of our first year asking simple questions like 'Why do we do it like that? Why don't we do it like this? Why has nobody ever mentioned that our non-alcoholic communion wine tastes so bad?!' It is interesting how many traditions an expectations can subtly become entrenched into our church culture. When discussed, some of those things can challenge people immensely, and issues such as worship styles, flowers or times of services can become central to what we value if w don't ever ask some difficult questions of ourselves. Tradition isn't necessarily bad of course, and patterns of worship are often significant and meaningful, but they *can* become more to do with external ceremony than inner purity or our purpose. It isn't always easy leading a church, but we thank God for our patient and passionate congregation who are still asking questions and growing in faith.

It was a simple question the Pharisees asked really. 'Why, Jesus, don't your disciples wash their hands before they eat as they should?' Jesus, however, turns their simple question into a deeper conversation, by answering their question with another question. He does a lot of that.

He challenges them about how they have adapted their own laws to suit their own purposes. He highlights how they have used a law that enables them to dedicate their possessions to God (but still use them themselves!) as an excuse not to obey the commandment to honour their father and mother. This pious loophole meant that their home was no longer available for caring for their elderly parents as it was consecrated to God. Jesus shines a spotlight on their hearts and clearly points out to them that no man-made law or tradition is so sacred that it trumps God's commandments and His heart for vulnerable people. Ouch!

Having questioned how genuine their adherence to the law is, Jesus then asks whether the 'tradition of the elders' matters most in this case anyway. These oral laws were the cumbersome added layers of regulations, which made it clear to see who was clean and who was not, and who was pleasing God and who was not. The truth is, it was easier to see who had washed their hands in an elaborate eating ritual than who had forgiven others or showed compassion to the poor. You can understand how that slope would get slippery. In their passion for purity, layers of extra duties kept getting added – just to make sure.

Jesus reminded them again, and He reminds us now – external behaviour doesn't always reveal our inner condition. Food, He said, goes in and it goes out again. But what spills out of our mouths – now *that* is more telling. We might not like to admit it, but we do sometimes put people down, tell lies, think lustfully, and behave immorally – maybe we too hope that God is distracted by our other good behaviour

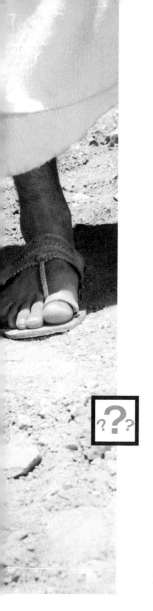

or that He just doesn't always notice that stuff. Frankly, we don't really like to acknowledge these habits or mistakes to ourselves, let alone to others or God.

Jesus asks us to shine a spotlight into our own hearts and to be scrupulously honest. As we survey our lives, Jesus reminds us that no amount of doing the right thing will make us right with God anyway. If it could, we would become insufferably smug and exhausted as well! Of course, attending church is important: serving, being generous and behaving appropriately all matter, but we can strip back beneath those things to remember, as it says in Romans 5:8, 'God demonstrates his own love for us in this: While we were still sinners, Christ died for us.' We can't impress others or God as a ticket into heaven, and we can't earn life in all its fullness. But we can be honest about our shortcomings, turn away from what is wrong, turn back to God and seek to live a life that responds to His love and sacrifice.

Discussion Starters

1. The Pharisees approached Jesus with a question. Jesus answered with a question. What do the questions we ask (to God and others) reveal about our own hearts and lives?

   _____

   _____

   _____

   _____

   _____

2. How do we make sure that the answers we give to each other go beyond the superficial into honesty? What are the obstacles to this?

   _____

   _____

   _____

   _____

   _____

3. The Pharisees had a passion for purity. They wanted to honour God in all of their lives, but the external signs had become their religion. Have you ever fallen into the trap of trying to be acceptable to God or a 'good Christian' by just doing more? What did that look like or feel like?

_____

_____

_____

_____

_____

4. How can we ensure that we partner with God to grow deeper in our faith as opposed to just trying harder or doing more?

_____

_____

_____

_____

_____

5. Read verses 13–14. How can we know what is 'planted by God' or which guides are leading us in the right direction?

_____

_____

_____

_____

_____

6. Have you experienced the Holy Spirit shining a light onto something in your life that needed to be challenged or changed? How did that make you feel? Why?

_____

_____

_____

_____

_____

7. Read verses 18–20. Which of these areas are more of an issue for you? Do we find certain temptations or challenges easier to talk about or confess to?

_____

_____

_____

_____

_____

8. This is a good time to take an individual spiritual audit. Give yourself a mark from 0–10 (10 is where you would like to be ultimately and 0 is not so good!) and try to pinpoint the reasons for this chosen mark.

_____

_____

_____

_____

_____

Final Thoughts

Every time we approach Jesus, we have another opportunity to look into our hearts and grow in our passion for purity. Jesus was never in the habit of trying to embarrass or guilt-trip people, and His Spirit is a wonderful counsellor in the way that God reveals His truth to us. God's love for us is complete and unconditional, and He loves us just as we are. He doesn't compare us to other people or expect us to be what we are not. But Jesus does ask us to be honest and vulnerable, and to seek to be all that we can uniquely be, in character and purpose.

And so, our heavenly Father, who knows what is in our hearts, lovingly challenges us when we need to adjust our focus. The result might not always be a predictable or easy life, but it will be a deeper and richer one. Indeed, as the Pharisees who approached Jesus heard, our faith must move beyond trying to be outwardly good or respectable enough, to knowing the heart of God and His grace. As Oswald

Chambers once helpfully said, 'Faith that is sure of itself is not faith; faith that is sure of God is the only faith there is.'

Closing Prayer

Lord, we thank You for Your wonderful Word. We thank You that we are saved by faith in You, and not by trying harder or by our outward appearances. We pray that as we make space for You, You will dwell in us richly by Your Spirit. We pray in Jesus' name. Amen.

Further Reflection

Listen to Matt Redman's song, *The Heart of Worship*. Let the words soak in as a response to all we have thought about. Take a moment to recommit your life to Jesus and His plans for you.

A Father:
A Persistent Prayer

Matthew 17:14–22

Warm Up

Children know what they want and are not afraid to ask for it again and again (and again!). Can you remember a present you desperately wanted for Christmas or a birthday when you were a child? What was it? Did you get it? How did that feel?

Opening Prayer

Lord, we thank You that we can come to You again and again with the things on our hearts. Thank You that You don't let us down, and You never let us go. Although we don't always know how You will answer us, we thank You that Your love for us is constant. We pray that we would come to You in faith, with a real yearning for more of Your power in our world. We believe that nothing is impossible with You. Amen.

Eye Opener

There have been many moments for me when only a cup of tea would do. Other times, I have been known to crave chocolate (okay, that's most of the time!). I have also experienced a longing to see somebody I love, and I have been fixated about something I want to purchase. I have been hungry both for food and for friendship. Sometimes, but not often enough, I am desperate for God, and persistent in prayer. This week, let's pull away from the distractions that fill our thoughts and open our eyes further to what God can do in us and through us.

Setting the Scene

Jesus was returning from the ultimate mountain top experience. He had just experienced the transfiguration, glowing white as light, meeting with Moses and Elijah and spectacularly reminding us of how He fulfils both the law and prophets. But just as when Moses came down the mountain from meeting with God (in Exod. 32) to see the inadequate

and chaotic faith of those who should know better, Jesus also comes back down to human messiness and spiritual confusion.

Isn't it often the case that after a spiritual high, we have a crashing reality check? But Jesus hadn't simply withdrawn up a mountain so that He could feel safe and close to God or to escape from reality. He retreated in order to know the presence of His Father and to hear His voice so that He, in turn, could then give His presence to those around Him and hear the voices of those who needed Him most. Time in the secret place equipped Him for the public place. We can learn so much from Him.

In the middle of the noisy crowd, a distraught father approaches Jesus. He is a desperate man. His son, who has seizures, needs a touch from Jesus. But, as usual, in this encounter, Jesus reveals as much about the spiritual condition of His followers as the physical condition of the boy.

Bible Readings

Matthew 17:14–21

When they came to the crowd, a man approached Jesus and knelt before him. 'Lord, have mercy on my son,' he said. 'He has seizures and is suffering greatly. He often falls into the fire or into the water. I brought him to your disciples, but they could not heal him.'

'You unbelieving and perverse generation,' Jesus replied, 'how long shall I stay with you? How long shall I put up with you? Bring the boy here to me.' Jesus rebuked the demon, and it came out of the boy, and he was healed from that moment.

Then the disciples came to Jesus in private and asked, 'Why couldn't we drive it out?'

He replied, 'Because you have so little faith. Truly I tell you, if you have faith as small as a mustard seed, you can say to this mountain, "Move from there to there," and it will move. Nothing will be impossible for you.'

Old Testament Connection
Daniel 3:17–18

If we are thrown into the blazing furnace, the God we serve is able to deliver us from it, and he will deliver us from Your Majesty's hand. But even if he does not, we want you to know, Your Majesty, that we will not serve your gods or worship the image of gold you have set up.

Session Focus

My heart goes out to the father in this passage. I am sure your's does too. He is a parent of a child with illness and special needs in a society with no medication, specialised schools, support or internet forums. This poor child has ended up in trauma and physical danger and his father is desperate. He had brought his child to the disciples believing they could help, and he had been disappointed. If only he could get to Jesus. You can sense the relief in the air when Jesus finally gets there.

When I have been ill, I have prayed and I have, of course, approached Jesus. But when one of my children has been really ill, and when my husband, Mark, was diagnosed with a disease that would rob him of his sight in his thirties (which it did) I didn't just approach Jesus – I, like the father in this passage, knelt down and repeatedly begged Jesus for mercy. I too have asked others to pray and I too have been disappointed. I can assure you that if Jesus was to physically turn up in my town today, I would grab Mark and I would elbow my way through the crowds until I found Him! Perhaps you can empathise?

This is a perplexing passage for all of us who are desperate for physical or mental healing or who pray earnestly for others in our family or our world. Jesus heals people, and yet sometimes our prayers are not apparently answered.

It is interesting that Jesus is clearly frustrated with His followers and their inability to engage their faith effectively. But, if I may sound a note of caution – my husband Mark and I have heard too many times that his blindness or perhaps another person's condition is due to our or their lack of faith. Let us note that it is not the child in this particular passage

19

that Jesus has asked more of, it is His disciples. How careful we must be not to add to the already heavy burden of the disabled, the depressed or the sick – Jesus loves them so much and would never wish them to live under that kind of pressure.

In the parallel passage in Mark 9, Jesus turns to the father and says that everything is possible for those who believe. And then we read in Mark 9:24: 'Immediately the boy's father exclaimed, "I do believe; help me overcome my unbelief!"' I don't know about you, but that is my cry so often! 'I do believe in You God, but I know I am only scratching the surface! Help me to know more of You!'

Jesus transformed the life of that child, and consequently the life of that desperate and trusting father. And thankfully, Jesus was also patient with His disciples, even though He challenged them to grow in their faith. He explained with deliberate exaggeration that the tiniest mustard seed of faith can move the biggest mountain of an obstacle. They had such little confidence in the divine authority invested into them and so little experience in exercising it. Perhaps we can relate to them too.

It is good to be reminded that just because life can be tough and demanding, it doesn't mean that God is. We must guard against the temptation to confuse life with God, or we will have a 'faith failure' whenever something bad happens. For all of us, it is undeniably easier to believe on the mountain, and much harder in the valley. This is why we need each other so much. Let's trust and support one another and bring each other to Jesus, avoiding the extremes of expecting every prayer to be answered as we demand, or never praying in case we are disappointed. We won't ever know about the faith of other people, and we are not to judge them anyway. But we are to approach Jesus with a longing for Him to move in the lives of those we care about, and we are called to employ whatever faith we have, knowing Jesus is patient and He is good, whatever the visible outcome.

Discussion Starters

1. What challenges would a parent of a sick or disabled child have had in Biblical times? Imagine the journey of that parent trying to find Jesus.

_____

_____

_____

_____

_____

2. Have you ever come to Jesus feeling desperate for Him to heal or to answer a particular prayer? Are you able to share the affect that issue had on you?

_____

_____

_____

_____

_____

3. Have you encountered the joy of experiencing God's healing or answers to prayer that have been life transforming?

_____

_____

_____

_____

_____

4. How do we cope with unanswered prayer or disappointment? Why do we so often face the temptation to explain or find reasons for it?

_____

_____

_____

_____

_____

5. Read Matthew 26:38–39. Jesus knew He was going to suffer and He prayed desperately. How does this passage encourage us as we face challenges or suffering?

_____

_____

_____

_____

_____

6. The words from the passage in Daniel demonstrate a faith in God whatever the outcome. How do we avoid confusing God with life?

_____

_____

_____

_____

_____

7. Find a picture of a mustard seed on the internet. It grows miraculously! How do we find the balance between praying with fixed expectations and not praying for fear of disappointment? How can we help each other?

_____

_____

_____

_____

_____

8. What different ways are there for us to pray for one another or people and situations we care about?

_____

_____

_____

_____

_____

Final Thoughts

The love of the father in this passage is so special and a great example to us. In a world where waiting for a microwave for a minute seems too much of a hassle, I wonder how often we have the kind of energy, love and sheer desperation that he displayed to persist in bringing people to Jesus. And yet we know so many situations and people that need His touch and restoration.

It is a real privilege to be able to turn our worries, concerns, desires, hopes, needs and heartbreaks into prayer. We can't possibly carry the hurt and frustration of our own lives, let alone the lives of those around us, on our own. And when we read the newspaper or hear about mission projects around the world, we know that we can approach Jesus and hold these situations and people out to Him. He has extraordinary compassion, and He will also help us to know how we should respond to the needs of the world. We can't fix every problem, but with God's help, we can be a part of bringing people towards Jesus and His all-sufficient grace. What an honour.

Closing Prayer

Lord, we thank You that You did not stay on a heavenly mountaintop, but that You chose to engage with our messy and difficult lives. We are sorry when we do not trust You or bring others to You; our heart's cry is that we believe, so we ask You to help our unbelief. Nothing is impossible with You Lord, and we trust that You are with us, both in the challenges and the joys. Amen.

Further Reflection

As you take time to reflect a little further, you might like to write or draw or just sit quietly to explore your thoughts.

Take some time to approach God and thank Him for the many times He has met us and answered prayer. It would be good to dwell on that and to grow our mustard seeds of faith and gratitude as a result.

Another way to approach Jesus is to lay down our disappointments and our desperate longings before Him and the cross. Spend some time asking for His power, but also for His reassurance and peace, which passes all understanding.

Peter: A Question of Forgiveness

Matthew 18:21–35

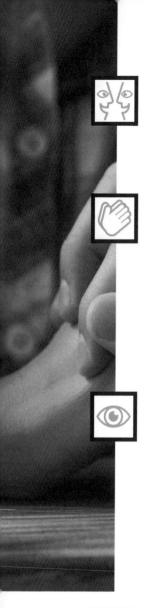

Warm Up

Discuss with your group (or consider, if you are alone) whether you are a 'hoarder' or a 'ditcher'. Do you keep things 'just in case' or for sentimental reasons, or are you unable to function if there is clutter in a drawer? How easy do you find it to let stuff go?

Opening Prayer

Lord, we approach You knowing that You are a merciful and forgiving God. We thank You again that despite our inadequacies, because of the death and resurrection of Jesus, we can come to You knowing forgiveness. We pray that at this moment, we would acknowledge and turn away from the things we know are wrong, and that You would enable us to extend the same forgiveness we receive to others. We can only pray this through the power of Jesus Christ our Lord. Amen.

Eye Opener

We all like to be forgiven, because we can't help getting things wrong!

I remember, when almost at the end of a long drive home one day, I was stopped by a police car. The speed limit had sneakily changed to 30mph at the bottom of the hill (where the camera sat waiting!) and I was still doing 34mph. That police officer had every right to issue me with a speeding ticket. That would have been justice. As it happened, he didn't, and in grateful response to his mercy I was probably a little more cautious and more generous to others on the road as well!

Setting the Scene

Although we all appreciate being forgiven, and in fact all have a real need to be forgiven, it is not always straightforward when we are called to forgive others. As I am sure you saw in the warm up, some people more naturally hold on to physical things and some people let them go more easily. But the same is true for emotional things and experiences too. Frankly, some people also have better memories than others. I am lucky if I can remember what happened before lunch and that can certainly help when I need to not hold a grudge!

Peter needed a lesson on forgiveness. I am so grateful for Peter and his tendency to blurt out questions, which we learn so much from. I am not sure what his brother Andrew had done to annoy him so much but he came to Jesus wanting to know how often he needed to forgive him. Actually, he quite amusingly came to Jesus with an answer to his own question. Rabbis taught that forgiving three times was the limit and so, having more than doubled that amount to seven, Peter probably reckoned he was being rather generous. But once again, when we come to Jesus with our questions and suggested answers, He does have a tendency to stretch our thinking and consequently open our hearts to much greater things.

Bible Readings

Matthew 18:21–35

Then Peter came to Jesus and asked, 'Lord, how many times shall I forgive my brother or sister who sins against me? Up to seven times?'

Jesus answered, 'I tell you, not seven times, but seventy-seven times.

'Therefore, the kingdom of heaven is like a king who wanted to settle accounts with his servants. As he began the settlement, a man who owed him ten thousand bags of gold was brought to him. Since he was not able to pay, the master ordered that he and his wife and his children and all that he had be sold to repay the debt.

'At this the servant fell on his knees before him. "Be patient with me," he begged, "and I will pay back everything." The servant's master took pity on him, cancelled the debt and let him go.

'But when that same servant went out, he found one of his fellow servants who owed him a hundred silver coins.

He grabbed him and began to choke him. "Pay back what you owe me!" he demanded.

'His fellow servant fell to his knees and begged him, "Be patient with me, and I will pay you back."

'But he refused. Instead, he went off and had the man thrown into prison until he could pay the debt. When the other servants saw what had happened, they were outraged and went and told their master everything that had happened.

'Then the master called the servant in. "You wicked servant," he said, "I cancelled all that debt of yours because you begged me to. Shouldn't you have had mercy on your fellow servant just as I had on you?" In anger his master handed him over to the jailers to be tortured, until he should pay back all he owed.

'This is how my heavenly Father will treat each of you unless you forgive your brother or sister from your heart.'

Old Testament Connection
Psalm 103:12

as far as the east is from the west, so far has he removed our transgressions from us.

Session Focus

Nelson Mandela is thought to have said that 'Resentment is like drinking poison and then hoping it will kill your enemies.' What inspiring words from a man who many would say had every good reason to be resentful, and to not practise forgiveness. Except Mandela knew that forgiveness is so much more than a fuzzy feeling – it is more like a daily decision to not be shackled to the past and to bitterness.

We can't wipe out what others have done to us, any more than we can erase our own mistakes. But we can ask for forgiveness and we can decide to forgive others irrespective of their own sense of guilt. Forgiveness is not about forgetting or minimizing events, it is about sifting our souls and finding a place of peace with God.

This passage is a powerful reminder of Matthew 6:14–16 where the Lord's prayer tells us to forgive others as we have been forgiven. And not just once or twice, or even seven times (poor Peter), but seventy-seven times which, more metaphorically, means as often as the need rises up in us to choose forgiveness over resentment.

Jesus explores what this means in this brilliant short story where the servant had been let off a huge debt, which amounted to more than an entire province earned – a vast amount – an unimaginable amount in fact. And yet he was not changed by it. He was living in the freedom of escaping prison, but he was not really free inside. Galatians 5:1 tells us: 'It is for freedom that Christ has set us free.' We are invited to live in the freedom of God's incredible mercy and forgiveness that has been extended to us. This servant, however? Well, he couldn't find it in himself to extend the same mercy to somebody who owed him a pittance. Matthew turns the story on its head and makes it very clear that we are not entitled to the kind of cheap grace that assumes we can be forgiven, while withholding that same grace from others.

Of course, there are times when the deeds we have to forgive feel far more than a pittance, and sometimes a good counsellor or a prayerful friend is the only way we can unknot the pain inside. So why then does Jesus make this such a priority when it can be so difficult? In fact, Jesus often chooses to focus on areas that are not always top of our agendas, like getting things out in the open, assessing our priorities, being humble and forgiving others. It seems that the key to living successfully is not in status or wealth, or even busy church services – it is in the richness of our relationships, with others and with God. Jesus is being very practical – He knows that in church and in life we will disagree and sometimes hurt each other. And just as forgiveness was the catalyst for our relationship with God, so it needs to be in the DNA of authentic Christian living.

I love to travel, and journeys, new horizons and fresh discoveries are exciting and interesting to me. Some of my best memories are from when I had experienced somewhere that looks and feels different. What a lot we would miss if instead of setting sail, we stayed anchored, bobbing around thinking that those harbour walls were in fact the horizon. It is tragic when there are heavy burdens of bitterness that we carry around, which hold us back when they could be dropped into the ocean of God's grace where we can trust that He knows what to do with them. It will take some space and time to let this happen, but we each need to keep taking the journey, letting the Spirit do His healing work in us.

God has exciting voyages ahead for us, things for us to see and explore as we live as forgiven and forgiving people who are really free.

Discussion Starters

1. What can we learn about Peter and his relationship with Jesus by the way he approaches Him in verse 21?

_____

_____

_____

_____

_____

2. What would be the advantages and disadvantages of having a set amount of times that we need to forgive somebody?

_____

_____

_____

_____

_____

3. Can you recall a time when somebody has forgiven you for something you have done? How did that impact you?

_____

_____

_____

_____

_____

4. What are your experiences of forgiving others? Is it something that comes naturally to you? How easily do you 'let things go'?

_____

_____

_____

_____

_____

5. What are the obstacles to forgiveness? Is there a sense that we don't want to let people off the hook, for example? How can we overcome these obstacles?

_____

_____

_____

_____

_____

6. In your experience of church, have you ever seen the results of broken relationships or unforgiveness?

_____

_____

_____

_____

_____

7. How often do we talk about how to deal with conflict and how and why we need to forgive one another?

_____

_____

_____

_____

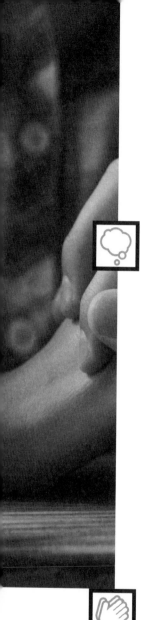

8. What 'journeys' might God be able to take us on when we know the freedom of right relationships? Use your imagination!

_____

_____

_____

_____

_____

Final Thoughts

Perhaps the only way we can truly find it in us to forgive others is to wrestle again and again with the incredible depth of forgiveness that we have received. Every day our list of ugly thoughts, missed opportunities, wrong choices, lazy words, and unkind actions just keeps increasing. I'm sure that's not just me! I'm so glad that people can't see the murky waters of my soul. I do so want to be more Christlike, but it's not a quick job. Do you think we sometimes forget how much we need the forgiveness of this holy but merciful God? Is it possible that because we don't have to bring rams or doves or perform elaborate rituals, which visually and powerfully remind us of our need for purification, that we forget what Jesus, the sacrificial Lamb, did for us?

The more that His grace and mercy overwhelms us, the more grace and mercy we will have to share. Forgiveness enables us to trust again and to be vulnerable in new ways; taking risks with people and opportunities, knowing that God has made a way for us to live authentic lives with Him and with others. Forgiveness is powerful.

Closing Prayer

Lord, we thank You for the cross. We thank You that when we approach You unsure of how we will keep forgiving, Your cross shows us the way. We know that in You we find freedom – from the wrong we have done and from the weight of the wrong that has hurt us. We thank You Jesus. Amen.

Further Reflection

Perhaps now or sometime this week you can take Communion with each other or with some friends or family. Or you might prefer to have a time of simply giving thanks alone or with others, perhaps with a candle to remind you that Jesus is the light of the world. Jesus knew we needed a way to remember, with all of our senses, what His death on the cross means to each of us. It doesn't have to be formal – the last supper was a meal with friends – but do take this opportunity to focus on how thankful you are for the forgiveness of Jesus and ask for His help to show His unconditional love to others.

A Rich Man and a Generous Woman: A Beautiful Thing

Matthew 19:16–26; 26:6–13

Warm Up

Stereotypes are a common but unfortunate part of everyday life, literature and entertainment. What descriptions do people think of (be honest!) when they hear the following words?
- Accountant
- Blonde
- Footballer
- Footballer's wife
- Politician
- Teenager
- Italian
- Librarian
- Any others?

Now, can you think of a real example for each of these where the stereotype is broken?

Opening Prayer

Lord, we thank You that You know us so completely. Sometimes we might jump to conclusions about others, but You know the whole story of people's lives. We thank You that You see past our status, gender and appearance, and we pray that whatever our background or circumstances, we would be generous with all that we have towards You. Amen.

Eye Opener

I have a sign above my cooker that reads: 'Dinner choices: 1 – Take it. 2 – Leave it.'

It never fails to make me laugh!

I am not exactly a domestic goddess, and I once heard my daughter telling guests that dinner would be ready when they heard the smoke alarm go off!

The thing is, people expect me to be good at this stuff as a church minister's wife (stereotyping!)... Or at least, I used to think they did. We expect certain people to behave in certain ways and when they don't, it can be surprising and challenging. In this study, we will meet two very different people who approached Jesus with unexpected results.

Setting the Scene

Imagine this very respectable man. He is extremely rich. Matthew tells us he is young. Luke tells us he is a ruler, a man with power. He is certainly confident, he is religious and he wants to know what he can do to live a good life that will gain him eternal and blessed results. Which of us in church leadership would not love somebody like *that* to turn up on a Sunday?

Imagine this woman. She arrives for a dinner with friends at a time where betrayal and controversy are looming outside. Without warning, she behaves so recklessly and so outrageously that almost everybody in the room is furious. She would hardly be what we would describe as a model church member, and would quite possibly provoke a pastoral crisis or two.

In both of these situations, as each of these people approach Jesus wanting to do something significant for different reasons, the disciples watch what is happening, get very confused and then learn something profound.

What about us? Is it possible that we allow the respectable and the predictable to become the acceptable in our Christian lives? When was the last time we really did something outrageous for Jesus?

Bible Readings

Matthew 19:16–26 (NIV 1984)

Now a man came up to Jesus and asked, 'Teacher, what good thing must I do to get eternal life?'

'Why do you ask me about what is good?' Jesus replied. 'There is only One who is good. If you want to enter life, obey the commandments.'

'Which ones?' the man enquired.

Jesus replied, '"Do not murder, do not commit adultery, do not steal, do not give false testimony, honour your father and mother" and "love your neighbour as yourself.'"

'All these I have kept,' the young man said. 'What do I still lack?'

Jesus answered, 'If you want to be perfect, go, sell your possessions and give to the poor, and you will have treasure in heaven. Then come, follow me.'

When the young man heard this, he went away sad, because he had great wealth.

Then Jesus said to his disciples, 'I tell you the truth, it is hard for a rich man to enter the kingdom of heaven. Again I tell you, it is easier for a camel to go through the eye of a needle than for a rich man to enter the kingdom of God.'

When the disciples heard this, they were greatly astonished and asked, 'Who then can be saved?'

Jesus looked at them and said, 'With man this is impossible, but with God all things are possible.'

Matthew 26:6–13
While Jesus was in Bethany in the home of Simon the Leper, a woman came to him with an alabaster jar of very expensive perfume, which she poured on his head as he was reclining at the table.

When the disciples saw this, they were indignant. 'Why this waste?' they asked. 'This perfume could have been sold at a high price and the money given to the poor.'

Aware of this, Jesus said to them, 'Why are you bothering this woman? She has done a beautiful thing to me. The poor you will always have with you, but you will not always have me. When she poured this perfume on my body, she did it to prepare me for burial. Truly I tell you, wherever this gospel is preached throughout the world, what she has done will also be told, in memory of her.'

Old Testament Connection
Proverbs 11:25
A generous person will prosper; whoever refreshes others will be refreshed.

Session Focus

Appearances can be deceptive. We were once members of a church with a marvellous church treasurer. He was gentle, a brilliant accountant (an actuary actually), sensible, smartly dressed, softly spoken, committed and a respectable man all round. As we got to know him however, we discovered something shocking and rather wonderful about him. This mild mannered man had a secret passion… for penguins! Cuddly penguins adorned his house. He even had his shower tiled with pictures of penguins. It was extraordinary! And it made us love him even more. That man and his wife modelled to us generosity, a love for people and sometimes a reckless commitment to God's kingdom.

Jesus knows what we are like beneath the surface, and whether our hearts are soft towards the kingdom of God, whatever our circumstances or social standing happen to be. For example, the rich young ruler thought he had it all sewn up. He lived a fabulous existence and the security of an eternal and blessed life would finish it off nicely, thank you very much. Perhaps he could do something noble and benevolent above the ordinary commandments – set up a charity or sponsor Jesus' next speaking tour perhaps. He was open to suggestions.

Now, Jesus didn't mind people being wealthy – He had other followers, like Zacchaeus and Nicodemus for example, who were undoubtedly well off. Certainly, in Jewish thinking, being rich was taken as a sign that you were blessed. Being rich isn't a sin – but it does come with danger. If we love things more than people, or spend more time worrying about protecting our standard of living than caring for others, that could prevent us from knowing a generosity of spirit and a freedom from the monster who always wants more. Jesus asks this rich young man to sell his belongings, give to the poor and then follow Him. When you have so much to surrender, those are three hard things to do. Tragically, he left with his bank balance intact but his soul deprived and the adventure of a life with Jesus behind him.

But the woman we meet later was a different story. Her extraordinary act of lavish generosity was described by

Jesus as 'a beautiful thing'. But how is this possible? He told the rich young ruler to give his money to the poor but now He is saying that this apparent waste of precious perfume was okay as the poor will always be here, but He won't be. It isn't that Jesus doesn't care about the poor – any reading of Scripture tells us that. But she was doing something significant. Her perfume was a scent used in burials, which had cost her dearly. Watched by a room of people including Lazarus (who had been raised from the dead), Simon (who presumably wasn't a leper anymore), and Judas (who was about to turn Jesus over for hard cash), she took the opportunity, which would never come around again, to show in the most prophetic and generous way possible, her love and respect for her Lord.

Sometimes God gives us a chance to do something extraordinary. To say something which will be remembered for decades. To be there for somebody at a crucial time. To sacrifice something which will leave a legacy for generations. To do 'something beautiful'. Jesus said that her heart and her actions would always be remembered. And it is so true – we always do remember those who have done extraordinary and generous things in our lives.

When we are prompted to do 'something beautiful' the chances are that it will probably cost us – our time, our money or our talents, and sometimes that cost will feel very high. Following Jesus was never supposed to be about making ourselves comfortable, but it doesn't exactly come naturally to us to make ourselves deliberately uncomfortable if we have a choice. Sometimes we might even walk away and regret a missed opportunity that may never come again. Other times, when we are prepared to take the risk, we might just get to do 'something beautiful' in the presence of Jesus.

Discussion Starters

1. How important are first impressions? How do we avoid stereotyping people?

_____

_____

_____

_____

_____

2. Have people ever jumped to conclusions about you? At work, college or church?

_____

_____

_____

_____

_____

3. Why do you think Jesus says it is harder for a rich person to enter heaven than for a camel to pass through the eye of a needle?

_____

_____

_____

_____

_____

4. Matthew 19:25–26 reassures us that it is possible for everybody to be saved. What part do we play in the story of salvation?

_____

_____

_____

_____

_____

5. Can you recall people who have done 'a beautiful thing' for you? What things stand out as beautiful?

_____
_____
_____
_____
_____

6. Are there times when you have felt great blessing as you have been generous? Have you any examples?

_____
_____
_____
_____
_____

7. Have we got any ideas about how to cope with living in such a consumerist society? How do we filter the constant adverts and messages about having more?

_____
_____
_____
_____
_____

8. How can we do 'something beautiful' for God and for others? Has God been prompting you to do something exciting or daunting? Can we help each other to step out in faith?

_____
_____
_____
_____
_____

Final Thoughts

Generosity is the best antidote I know to living in our society where we often think that 'enough' is just a little bit more than we have now...

Whether it is our time, our possessions or how we invest in our relationships, there is a constant tension between wanting to fulfil ourselves and wanting to serve others. It isn't that God wants us all to be poor and exhausted, always at the beck and call of other people. He asks us to be wise and to be good stewards. Jesus spent a lot of time talking about managing our possessions, our priorities and modelling a life of love.

God desires that we are free to be able to follow Him, to be outrageously generous and hospitable, to go to places we hadn't expected, to serve people we didn't know existed and to be able to make choices that reflect the kingdom of God. And whatever obstacles hold us back from that – whether it is the love of money, people, self-absorption, doubt, fear or respectability – then He will ask us whether we would lay it down and follow Him first. Humanly speaking, this looks impossible, but with God's help it is possible.

Closing Prayer

We thank You Lord, that whether we have a lot or a little, You ask us to trust and follow You. We thank You that a life with You is unpredictable and exciting. We pray that in Your name we would do many generous and beautiful things and see many lives transformed. Amen.

Further Reflection

Listen to the song *Living for Your Glory* by Tim Hughes.
If you have the chance, listen to it more than once.

As you listen, let the words become your words and
offer yourself in worship, open to how the Lord might lead
your thoughts.

Write down and pray over anything that He might be
speaking to you about.

Is He asking you to do something beautiful?

Judas: A Hidden Agenda
Matthew 26:47-54

Warm Up

Place an object like a cup or a rock where you can see it. How many different uses for this item can you think of? If you are in a group – split into teams and see who can think of the most uses! You might have to think laterally!

Opening Prayer

Lord, we pray that we would see life more and more from Your perspective. We are sorry if we ask You to bless our plans instead of finding out Your purposes. As we come to You again, we worship You, we thank You and we declare that we want eyes to see and ears to hear Your voice above all else. In Jesus' name we pray. Amen.

Eye Opener

Recently my family and I watched a romantic comedy film. Towards the end came the inevitable and dramatic kiss and it was fascinating to see how differently we all responded. My oldest teenage daughter thought it was 'soooo' romantic. My younger daughter thought it was plain awkward and hid behind a cushion. I panicked about whether it was going to be appropriate viewing and I am sure my husband wondered when he could swap channels to watch a show about cars. Who would have thought that a kiss could be seen in so many different ways?

Setting the Scene

The passage for this study is a scripture that might well stop us in our tracks. Of all the people who approached Jesus in all of the Gospels, this is probably the most dramatic moment of them all, and in many ways the most heartbreaking.

Jesus has just spent a soul-searching and painful time of prayer and sorrow in the garden of Gethsemane, and knows that the path ahead will involve suffering and rejection.

It will not be easy. Even His closest friends are sleepy, impetuous, or about to deny Him. At this dark moment, one of those very close disciples, Judas, approaches Him. And he does so with a kiss – a kiss described in the original language as warm and affectionate, but a kiss with a bitter aftertaste of betrayal.

Everybody present at that scene would have seen that kiss from their own perspective. The disciples would have seen one thing; the arriving crowd of 'police' sent by the plotting chief priest another. Judas had his own agenda and Jesus – well, Jesus could see what was happening in the hearts of everybody around Him.

And while each person had a unique part to play in the unfolding tragedy, Jesus, who looked like a victim in the plot, was actually in control. He could have performed a hundred powerful miracles and silenced them all, but He refused to. He had His own perspective and a heavenly agenda to pursue.

Bible Readings

Matthew 26:47–54

While he was still speaking, Judas, one of the Twelve, arrived. With him was a large crowd armed with swords and clubs, sent from the chief priests and the elders of the people. Now the betrayer had arranged a signal with them: 'The one I kiss is the man; arrest him.' Going at once to Jesus, Judas said, 'Greetings, Rabbi!' and kissed him.

Jesus replied, 'Do what you came for, friend.'

Then the men stepped forward, seized Jesus and arrested him. With that, one of Jesus' companions reached for his sword, drew it out and struck the servant of the high priest, cutting off his ear.

'Put your sword back in its place,' Jesus said to him, 'for all who draw the sword will die by the sword. Do you think I cannot call on my Father, and he will at once put at my disposal more than twelve legions of angels? But how then would the Scriptures be fulfilled that say it must happen this way?'

Old Testament Connection
Isaiah 53:7
He was oppressed and afflicted, yet he did not open his mouth;

he was led like a lamb to the slaughter, and as a sheep before its shearers is silent, so he did not open his mouth.

Session Focus

There are times when we feel an emotion with such passion or force that it seems impossible to us that other people cannot read our minds simply by being in our presence. Certainly, it is a constant frustration to me that those closest to me are not always able to pick up on my mental messages! Likewise, sometimes we are not very successful at interpreting the thoughts or actions of those around us, we might even make assumptions or attribute certain attitudes or character traits to them, sometimes positive, and sometimes not.

At our church we often talk about the OFM principle – meaning One Fact More. We so often would see things differently with One crucial Fact More. Could, for example, that person who seems so abrasive at the moment actually be bearing the weight of bereavement? Or perhaps that other person who doesn't reply to our call – maybe their mobile phone is lost? It does pay to give people the benefit of the doubt sometimes, as we would quite definitely like it if they did the same for us! The truth is, there are always other perspectives that we are simply not aware of.

So, who knows exactly what was going through Judas' mind. We don't have the privilege of being able to ask for One Fact More about Judas as he approached Jesus with a kiss and his own hidden agenda. Was it that Jesus had simply not turned out to be the kind of Messiah he'd hoped for? Did he still long for a revolutionary leader who would rid Palestine of Roman domination? Did he perhaps hope that by placing Jesus in this confrontational situation that Jesus would finally call on the power of heaven and turn everything upside down? Or was it simply about the money?

Whatever his thinking, he had made a calculated and deliberate choice. Sometimes we mess up and sin impulsively

or thoughtlessly, but the humbling truth is that we also have the capacity to decide to behave in a dark and premeditated way. As Judas watched his Master and Friend led away, he was confronted with the terrible belief that he could not live with what he had done. It is tragic reading; this once friend of Jesus throwing the blood money back into the Temple, protesting Jesus' innocence and then finally ending his own life.

But at the same time, Peter was navigating his own way through the same circumstances. He would be defending Jesus with a sword one minute (John explains it was Peter who did the ear chopping) and then denying Him the next. He was going to be the rock on whom God would build the future Church – but frankly, it was going to be a rocky road for a while.

Jesus knew about Judas and He knew about Peter. He also knew about the manipulative and hard heart of Caiaphas, the high priest, and the Pharisees who were plotting His arrest. But, with a perspective that nobody fully appreciated, He also knew that He was about to fulfil the prophecies of generations and the purposes of the Father for broken people everywhere.

He alone could see from every angle.

If we look into our hearts, is it possible that similarly to Judas, we sometimes are driven by our own agendas and even try to force the hand of Jesus? We would love for Him to behave or react as we think would be best. But, of course, we can't use God for our purposes, and we do not know better than our Maker.

Is it also possible that, like Peter, we sometimes overreact to circumstances, violently defensive one moment, in denial another and broken by repentance soon after. But our emotions are not supposed to be the centre of our lives– we need to pause and find the wisdom that comes from seeing what Jesus is revealing.

We are all so different. We all have our own strengths and weaknesses, our own insecurities and desires for significance or status. Many of us have been driven by the desire to be loved or a need to be right. And consequently we will all approach Jesus in our own complex way. How wonderful that Jesus has far more than One Fact More about us; He knows us intimately and loves us unconditionally, and He wants us to know Him more.

Discussion Starters

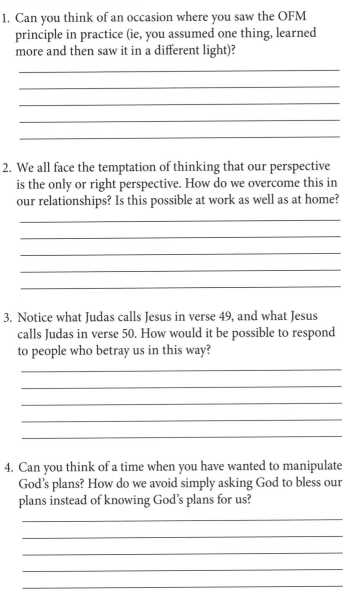

1. Can you think of an occasion where you saw the OFM principle in practice (ie, you assumed one thing, learned more and then saw it in a different light)?

_____

_____

_____

_____

_____

2. We all face the temptation of thinking that our perspective is the only or right perspective. How do we overcome this in our relationships? Is this possible at work as well as at home?

_____

_____

_____

_____

_____

3. Notice what Judas calls Jesus in verse 49, and what Jesus calls Judas in verse 50. How would it be possible to respond to people who betray us in this way?

_____

_____

_____

_____

_____

4. Can you think of a time when you have wanted to manipulate God's plans? How do we avoid simply asking God to bless our plans instead of knowing God's plans for us?

_____

_____

_____

_____

_____

5. Are you a person who responds to situations particularly emotionally? How can those of us who feel deeply avoid seeing everything through our emotions?

_____
_____
_____
_____
_____

6. Are you a person who responds to situations particularly logically? How can those of us who like everything to make sense avoid seeing everything too analytically?

_____
_____
_____
_____
_____

7. Why is it important that Jesus fulfils the Old Testament scriptures (eg v54)?

_____
_____
_____
_____
_____

8. What does this passage reveal to you about Jesus that is particularly interesting or new in some way?

_____
_____
_____
_____
_____

Final Thoughts

I recently heard somebody say that wisdom is 'knowing what to do, when you don't know what to do'. I thought that was very wise! Wisdom is also knowing that you might not always know what to do, but there are always others who know more than you who could help. Most of all, wisdom is knowing that God does know what to do, and also cares deeply about how we are to be. He is, after all, wonderfully above our plans, our motives, agendas and our limited perspective on life.

How marvellous it would be to see more of God's wisdom in our stressful situations. How transforming it would be to know Him right at the centre of our relationships. How inspiring it would be to sense Him in more of our hopes and ambitions. How comforting it would be to know more of His presence in our fears and our suffering.

As we approach Jesus and seek Him more, we will increasingly see from His perspective as we think of others and of situations around us. It is in His presence that He reveals to us the significant role He has for us to play in His unfolding story in the world.

Closing Prayer

Lord, we thank You that through Your Spirit we can grow in wisdom and truth. Even if we betray You with our actions or deny You with our words, You will always welcome us back and give us a future. Holy Spirit, come. Refresh us and give us a heavenly perspective as we look around us each day. Amen.

Further Reflection

You might already know these verses in Proverbs 3:5–6: 'Trust in the LORD with all your heart and lean not on your own understanding;

in all your ways submit to him, and he will make your paths straight.'

Let these verses penetrate your heart and mind by doing something creative with them: paint or write out the words, design and print them out, or express them in a poem or song. Perhaps you could place them somewhere significant.

While exploring the verses, take time to meditate about areas of your life or different relationships with the words in mind.

Mary and Mary:
A Restoration Project

Matthew 28:1-10

Warm Up

Take a picture from a newspaper or magazine that has been cut into many pieces. Take turns putting a piece back into the picture until it is fully restored. How easy was the process and how did you feel afterwards?

Opening Prayer

Lord, we are in awe of You once again. We worship You and thank You for Your incredible sacrifice for us. We are witnesses to the power of Your resurrection and Your ability to make all things new. We thank You that we are a vital part of Your story of hope and restoration for this world that You love so much. Amen.

Eye Opener

So far during our married life my husband and I have owned five houses and renovated them all. I am not quite sure why we love a 'fixer-upper' so much. Perhaps it is the price and the ability to afford what would be beyond our reach without hard work, or maybe it is the opportunity to shape something as we would like it to be. But, without a doubt, seeing the potential is exciting. Restoring a tired building into something welcoming, beautiful and personal to us is a genuine pleasure. Seeing something once neglected brought back to life is a rewarding and creative process.

Setting the Scene

Finally, the authorities had Jesus exactly where they wanted Him – dead and buried – with guards and a heavy stone just to be doubly sure that there would be no funny business from those pesky disciples.

But can you imagine what a confusing, grief stricken and dark time that must have been for the men and women who had known and loved Jesus? It must have seemed like they were fumbling with the scattered pieces of their lives

– a jumbled jigsaw with no finished picture to help them and no obvious way of the puzzle fitting together anymore. They were, I would guess, afraid and unsure about their future. This was not what it was all supposed to look like in their minds.

How many of us have felt like that – afraid and unsure; surveying the circumstances around us in our lives or in the world and unsure of where to put our faith or how to move forwards? There's no way around it, we will all reach that point from time to time.

How wonderful to know that this was not the end of the road for the disciples, and it isn't for us either. Our faith depends on the resurrection and its power to restore hope, renew minds and rebuild lives. Only Jesus could reconcile us to God in the way that He did, and in doing so, He creates a new picture – a new vision of our life and our world.

Bible Readings

Matthew 28:1–9

After the Sabbath, at dawn on the first day of the week, Mary Magdalene and the other Mary went to look at the tomb.

There was a violent earthquake, for an angel of the Lord came down from heaven and, going to the tomb, rolled back the stone and sat on it. His appearance was like lightning, and his clothes were white as snow. The guards were so afraid of him that they shook and became like dead men.

The angel said to the women, 'Do not be afraid, for I know that you are looking for Jesus, who was crucified. He is not here; he has risen, just as he said. Come and see the place where he lay. Then go quickly and tell his disciples: "He has risen from the dead and is going ahead of you into Galilee. There you will see him." Now I have told you.'

So the women hurried away from the tomb, afraid yet filled with joy, and ran to tell his disciples. Suddenly Jesus met them. 'Greetings,' he said. They came to him, clasped his feet and worshipped him.

Old Testament Connection
Isaiah 49:8–9

This is what the LORD says:

'In the time of my favour I will answer you, and in the day of salvation I will help you;

I will keep you and will make you to be a covenant for the people,

to restore the land and to reassign its desolate inheritances,

to say to the captives, "Come out," and to those in darkness, "Be free!"'

Session Focus

Following Jesus is an invitation to expect the unexpected. I am sure the disciples must have felt bewildered many times as they followed Him – asking Him questions, witnessing Him perform miracles, watching Him as He challenged the respectable and fraternized with the undesirable.

But a resurrection from the dead? Nobody was expecting that. That was definitely not on the cards. But nothing about Jesus was expected – He had lived an unexpected life – born in an insignificant place, in the family carpentry trade and hung on a cross in the place of disgrace with common criminals. This was nothing like a saviour as they had imagined He would be.

As if to reinforce this point even further, Jesus revealed His resurrection first to Mary and Mary – women who could not even speak in a court of law, who were not trusted as witnesses and who were, in many ways, seen as insignificant in their society. This was both extraordinary and profound. Can you imagine these two faithful women approaching Jesus in the tomb, only to discover in the most startling way that He was not there; He was already ahead of them? Jesus was no longer in their place of grief, He was ahead, in an unexpected place of joy where they could approach Him again and discover a new future.

The power of the resurrection is still wonderfully at work in lives across the world. Like Mary and Mary, He takes the most unqualified of us and uses us to teach others. He turns words of criticism or expectation upside down into promises of acceptance and hope. He takes the wisdom of the world and spins it on its axis until it is revealed as foolishness. He takes those who feel discarded, overlooked, judged, misunderstood, shameful or just plain tired and offers us the hope that He can make all things new.

He is also ahead of us. Of course Jesus wants us to approach Him exactly as we are; but then, as He reveals more of His grace and power to us, He also leads us forwards with Him as our guide. Just as the grave couldn't keep Him, even our cold, dark places of sadness and doubt can also find the warmth of new life with the help of His Holy Spirit.

Of course, restoration of a house or an antique isn't something that happens instantly or without some perseverance; it takes patience and commitment to see the grubby layers rubbed back to reveal the beauty beneath. Certainly, in our experience of house restoration, there have been times when we have wondered whether we could persevere any longer with the work and expense involved.

But Jesus is in the people restoration business. He renamed Peter the 'rock' on whom He would build His Church (who would have thought?), and transformed James and John, known as 'sons of thunder' into apostles of love. Thankfully Jesus is just as passionately committed to seeing you and I restored into all that God wants us to be, and is more patient about the process than we would ever be!

Each day, as we approach God again, we can have confidence that He is the Master Craftsman who can continually restore and reshape us as He leads us into new opportunities to share faith, hope and love with others.

This restoration story is the wonder of the kingdom of God – as unexpected as it is! Because of Jesus, we are reconciled to God and transformed by His grace. No wonder the Marys' and the disciples' first reaction was to worship. And no wonder the conclusion to this encounter and to the Gospel of Matthew was to for them to go and share this wonderful news and to make more disciples with the promise that Jesus would always be with them.

That's our mission, and the promise He has for us too. His compassion for His world has not changed, and He

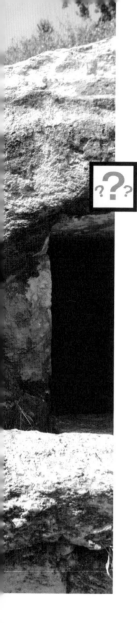

leads us ahead to bring freedom to the oppressed, food to the hungry, comfort to the weak and hope to the hopeless. What an amazing restoration project that is!

Discussion Starters

1. Briefly share any restoration projects you have been a part of. What was that experience like?

_____

_____

_____

_____

_____

2. Consider the renovation or maintenance of a house. Is it ever finished? What can we learn about our own spiritual journey by using this as an analogy for our lives?

_____

_____

_____

_____

_____

3. What are some of the emotions and thoughts that Mary and Mary must have experienced as they approached the tomb that morning? Try and imagine their conversation on the way there.

_____

_____

_____

_____

_____

4. In verse 9, when the women are approached by Jesus, they came to Him and worshipped Him. Have there been tough times in your life where you have unexpectedly met with Jesus? How does this affect your worship of Him?

_____
_____
_____
_____
_____

5. What does knowing the power of the resurrection mean for us as individuals and in our church?

_____
_____
_____
_____
_____

6. How do we keep the power of the cross and resurrection at the heart of our faith and our life?

_____
_____
_____
_____
_____

7. What areas of influence has God given you? How are you to bring restoration and re-creation to people, circumstances, or the environment?

_____
_____
_____
_____
_____

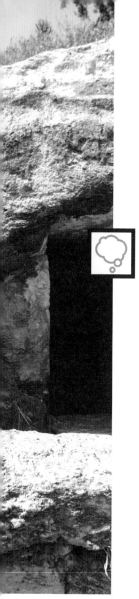

8. Are there other areas you sense that God is asking you to invest your life in? It could be at church or further afield. He loves to ask us to do unexpected things!

_____

_____

_____

_____

_____

Final Thoughts

Even if you have never restored a piece furniture or renovated a house, you have probably at some point completed a jigsaw puzzle. All of these images reveal a little to us of God's desire to interact with His world, patiently and lovingly re-creating value and beauty. The wonderful truth is that each of us is a vital part in this process – bringing the compassion and hope of the kingdom of God in practical and personal ways. God cares for His people and the planet we live on, and asks us to join with Him in restoring his creation, and reconciling people to each other and to Him.

Our lives are a demonstration of a living, loving and forgiving faith. Our churches and homes are places that, with God's help, can display an example of life lived a different way – God's way. We may not be perfect (restoration is complicated and messy!), but like Mary and Mary who approached Jesus both on the cross and as our resurrected Lord, we can have confidence that He is still at work in us and through us today.

Closing Prayer

Lord, we thank You for giving Your life for us on the cross. We approach You, knowing You forgive us and make all things new. We thank You for the empty tomb, the hope of a new and purposeful life, and the promise of eternal life. May Your resurrection power continue to transform us, and others through us. In Your powerful name we pray, Amen.

Further Reflection

Reflect upon the areas where you are praying that God will bring new life and new hope. You might want to look at a cross and/or a stone representing the empty tomb to remind you of the power of the cross and the resurrection.

Where in your personal life, your church ministry or your concern for the world, would you long to see God move in power, restoring and building His kingdom and His purposes?

Listen to the song *Beautiful Things* by Gungor and bring these places and people to God in your mind, thanking Him for His goodness to us.

Leader's Notes

General Notes on Leading the Studies

The aim of these six studies is for us to approach Jesus again (both as individuals and as groups) as we look through the eyes of people who approached Jesus in the Gospel of Matthew.

I hope you will find these studies to be both practical and personal, combining honesty and humour with biblical study. I hope and pray that this will echo into the group you are leading as you share the studies.

Of course, the level of vulnerability you achieve in your group often reflects the extent to which the leader is prepared to share their own experiences and insights – so I am praying for you – that you will be inspired and encouraged personally as you prepare to lead others towards Jesus in the days ahead.

The warm up sections might take you a very short time to prepare in advance. The reflection at the end might also necessitate you finding the piece of music online or on a CD.

Each session includes more reading and questions than are probably feasible to cover in an average length small group gathering. I would strongly recommend that each member of the group is encouraged to use this guide himself or herself throughout the week, adding their own answers and insights as preparation for your time together. They could write in this guide or use a journal as part of their individual spiritual development. This way, you will have more time for the questions and you can choose to focus on the readings or questions that you particularly feel are helpful for your group.

The following notes are ideas and guidance to help you navigate certain questions or sections. May God bless you as you approach Jesus and lead others into His presence.

STUDY ONE: The Pharisees: A Passion for Purity

Warm Up
Sweets such as Maltesers® or peppermint creams would work well, and a pomegranate or a pineapple would be ideal for fruit.

Discussion Starters
Question 1: Sometimes our questions concern our own needs, and sometimes our questions are all about other people. Some people lean towards one of these – we probably all do at different times. What we ask might reveal something of our emotional and spiritual condition at that time.

Questions 6 and 7: These questions create an opportunity for you to share more personally together. There might be some very honest things shared, or people might feel more cautious. Try to draw the conversation in from the general into real examples – without making people feel unnecessarily uncomfortable. An example from your own life might help.

Question 8: This is a chance for your group to reflect much more privately and to be able to be totally honest before God.

Reflection
You can find this song on YouTube, Spotify or CD.

STUDY TWO: A Father: A Persistent Prayer

Discussion Starters

Question 2 and 4: You will probably find a wide variety of responses to these questions. Some people will talk about asking God for a job, a child, healing or a reconciliation, for example. Some of these might be quite difficult to share. Take time to make sure that everybody is heard. Rejoice with those who have seen God answer prayer but in question 4, help the group to avoid giving easy answers or explanations in their desire to be kind. As the questions suggest – sometimes the main thing is to share these experiences and feelings and to bring them to God without trying to rationalize them.

Question 6: Daniel's friends did not know the outcome as they approached the furnace, or whether they would live or die. But they prayed in faith and declared that either way their faith in God would not be affected.

Question 8: How creative can we be with our prayer life as a group or as individuals? We could do some helpful research into creative prayers and different prayer tools and resources. It might be that as a group we could create a bank of ideas to deepen and extend our prayer life.

Reflection

If you have time to do this as a group, this would be an ideal time to put into practice some creative prayer – you could write prayers of thanks on a printed rainbow or picture of a mustard tree for the first half of the reflection, or use pebbles or pieces of paper to place our burdens down before a cross for the second half, for example.

STUDY THREE: Peter: A Question of Forgiveness

Discussion Starters

Question 4 and 5: It is difficult to forgive others. Some people may have been wronged on a very great scale and find forgiveness an ongoing and painful process. While we need to avoid giving people permission to withhold forgiveness, it is also okay to acknowledge that it is not always possible to find forgiveness a simple and immediate matter and to validate their feelings. It might be that some people need more support outside the group to work through some issues.

Question 6: This question is not designed to encourage people to share any general dissatisfaction with the Church or disparaging experiences about other members of the Church! There is not a church in the world that gets everything right of course. However, it is good to appropriately acknowledge and learn from times when we have been disappointed by others. We all need to learn that while others may disappoint us, God is still faithful. We have a chance to model, extend and experience forgiveness in a way that marks us out as the community of God; sometimes that happens well, sometimes it doesn't. Can we help each other to grow in this?

Question 8: When we find freedom through forgiveness, we open our hearts and minds to all kinds of possibilities. We can trust again, love again, take risks, open our minds to new serving opportunities and assert ourselves at work, for example. When we hold back forgiveness, cynicism and anxiety are examples of the kind of obstacles that might stop us from living this adventure of faith. Only the freedom found through giving and receiving the forgiveness of Christ can give us hope.

Reflection

If appropriate, share Communion or encourage people to do so during the week. For some, it might be more appropriate to have a time of thanksgiving and prayer using a candle to

focus them. Sharing either of these together demonstrates how Jesus uses our senses to impress into our hearts and minds the truths about His goodness and His sacrifice.

STUDY FOUR: A Rich Man and a Generous Woman: A Beautiful Thing

Warm Up
Hopefully you *will* find an example to counteract each of these stereotypes – you could always prepare some to be sure!

Discussion Starters
Question 3: Bear in mind that, relatively speaking, we are probably all quite wealthy. If we have our own front door, cupboards with food, education and medicine we are wealthier than a great deal of the world. It is easy to discount ourselves when we see others with even more money, but all of us should examine the hold that possessions and status have on us.

Question 7: This might well be one of the most important questions we can answer living in a culture that promotes the cult of 'me' and 'my comfort' above almost everything else. We are called to be disciples not consumers – but consumerism is the pool of culture that we are swimming in every day. Do we even realize how much it impacts us?

Question 8: If given enough time – this question could be the catalyst for some really Spirit-led blessing. Who could God bless and encourage as we prayerfully wait and seek His guidance? This might be something to follow up another time. We can encourage each other to turn our intentions into actions.

Reflection
This song can be found on YouTube, Spotify or on CD – the original is found on Tim Hughes' album *Holding Nothing Back*, but it is also on the *Living for Your Glory: Soul Survivor Live 2007* CD and others.

STUDY FIVE: Judas: A Hidden Agenda

Discussion Starters

Questions 1 and 2: We all have a tendency to think we are right. Our greatest blind spot is usually ourselves after all! When we speak to a spouse, a child, a friend or a colleague, we can train ourselves in empathy by really trying to see things from their perspective, and to ask questions. Encourage the group to engage the OFM principle for the week ahead. You could share by text message, Facebook group or email any examples where this has had an impact. We have frequently been surprised by the power of this principle.

Questions 5 and 6: Clearly, there is not a right or wrong kind of personality. Each person will have strengths and weaknesses to the way they approach life, relationships and conflict. The idea here is to become increasingly self-aware about how our 'shape' affects our interaction with others, and how increasing awareness of others can change our relationships too. Do affirm each other as you grow in understanding about each other.

Reflection

Depending on time and the dynamics of your group, you could create something together – like a collage or a psalm where you take turns writing a line using the letters of the alphabet as the beginning of each line. It may be more feasible to encourage people to carve out some time to create something on their own. Some people don't think they are creative, but we are all designed in the image of the Creator God! Some people will work better with words, some with images, some with technology like PowerPoint or photography. Some people could share these expressions of these verses next time, others might prefer to keep them private. The emphasis is not on the quality of artistry – it is on the process of expressing and exploring the meaning of the verses.

STUDY SIX: Mary and Mary: A Restoration Project

Warm Up

Find a nice big picture from a magazine and stick it to some cardboard to make the paper thicker. Then cut it up into pieces in advance – not too tiny or you will be there all night – but enough pieces to make it a challenge!

Discussion Starters

Question 4: We all experience God in unexpected ways and the ways that God speaks at those times are seemingly endless. Some examples might be a card from somebody, some words that are deeply significant, a timely rainbow, a verse that absolutely shouts from the pages of the Bible, a sense of reassurance, a turn of events that surprise us or an image or scene which speaks to us profoundly. It might take a few moments to recall some of these instances.

Question 7: We have all been placed by God into relationships, circumstances and locations where God wants to use us. It can be very powerful to acknowledge these as spheres of influence and mission. We can be pastors of our home, street, playground or office. As a group, it is great to be intentional about becoming more aware of these places in each other's life and to be able to pray for the places where we would like to see His kingdom come and His will be done.

Question 8: There are, in most people, spoken or unspoken nudges towards the homeless, the poor, the disabled, the oppressed, the lonely, the young or perhaps toward certain places. The heart of God towards them often draws our own hearts in response. For each of us, that compassion will be expressed in different ways – by supporting charities or people financially or in prayer, or by stepping out into serving in new and exciting ways. This might either feel risky or straightforward. God could ignite our imagination about how He might use us further to bring hope and restoration.

Commit to exploring and researching any of these nudges and to keep praying into how they might be expressed. Affirm each other and encourage each other as you share.

Reflection

Consider how you might connect with this reflection in a way that is a meaningful for you. Would something creative be helpful or writing your prayer? Or perhaps a prolonged time of quiet would help. The cross and/or the stone may well stimulate your prayers as you approach Jesus with faith, hope and love.

You can find this song on YouTube, Spotify or on CD. The original is found on the Gungor CD of the same name, *Beautiful Things*. There are some examples of this song on YouTube that have been set to images, which might be helpful as the song powerfully expresses the hope that our Saviour can make things new and beautiful.

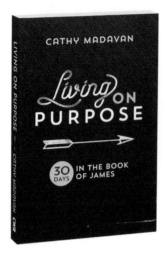

SmallGroup central

All of our small group ideas and resources in one place

Online:

www.smallgroupcentral.org.uk
is filled with free video teaching,
tools, articles and a whole host
of ideas.

On the road:

A range of seminars themed for
small groups can be brought to
your local community. Contact us at
hello@smallgroupcentral.org.uk

In print:

Books, study guides and DVDs
covering an extensive list of themes,
Bible books and life issues.

Log on and find out more at:
www.smallgroupcentral.org.uk

Courses and events

Waverley Abbey College

Publishing and media

Conference facilities

Transforming lives

CWR's vision is to enable people to experience personal transformation through applying God's Word to their lives and relationships.

Our Bible-based training and resources help people around the world to:
• Grow in their walk with God
• Understand and apply Scripture to their lives
• Resource themselves and their church
• Develop pastoral care and counselling skills
• Train for leadership
• Strengthen relationships, marriage and family life and much more.

Our insightful writers provide daily Bible reading notes and other resources for all ages, and our experienced course designers and presenters have gained an international reputation for excellence and effectiveness.

CWR's Training and Conference Centre in Surrey, England, provides excellent facilities in an idyllic setting – ideal for both learning and spiritual refreshment.

CWR Applying God's Word
to everyday life and relationships

CWR, Waverley Abbey House,
Waverley Lane, Farnham,
Surrey GU9 8EP, UK

Telephone: **+44 (0)1252 784700**
Email: **info@cwr.org.uk**
Website: **www.cwr.org.uk**

Registered Charity No. 294387
Company Registration No. 1990308